SO-AHU-076

Livonia Public Library
ALFRED NOBLE BRANCH
32901 PLYMOUTH ROAD
Livonia, Michigan 48150-1793
(734)421-6600
LIVN #19

# PATRIOTS IN PETTICOATS

## HEROINES OF THE
## AMERICAN REVOLUTION

# PATRIOTS IN PETTICOATS

## HEROINES OF THE
## AMERICAN REVOLUTION

## SHIRLEY RAYE REDMOND

Landmark Books®

Random House New York

Livonia Public Library
ALFRED NOBLE BRANCH
32901 PLYMOUTH ROAD
Livonia, Michigan 48150-1793
(734)421-6600
LIVN #19

Copyright © 2004 by Shirley Raye Redmond. All rights reserved
under International and Pan-American Copyright Conventions.
Published in the United States by Random House Children's Books,
a division of Random House, Inc., New York, and simultaneously in
Canada by Random House of Canada Limited, Toronto.

www.randomhouse.com/kids

*Library of Congress Cataloging-in-Publication Data*
Redmond, Shirley Raye.
Patriots in petticoats : heroines of the American Revolution /
by Shirley Raye Redmond.
p.   cm. — (Landmark books)
SUMMARY: Profiles girls and women who participated in the American
Revolution by refusing to buy British merchandise, collecting money,
and even going to war as wives, nurses, spies, or soldiers.
ISBN 0-375-82357-3 (trade) — ISBN 0-375-92357-8 (lib. bdg.)
1. United States—History—Revolution, 1775–1783—Women—Juvenile
literature. 2. United States—History—Revolution, 1775–1783—Participation,
Female—Juvenile literature. 3. United States—History—Revolution,
1775–1783—Biography—Juvenile literature. 4. Women—United States—
Biography—Juvenile literature. 5. Women heroes—United States—
Biography—Juvenile literature. [1. United States—History—Revolution,
1775–1783—Women. 2. United States—History—Revolution,
1775–1783—Participation, Female. 3. Women—Biography.]
I. Title.    E276.R43  2004  973.3'082—dc21  2003004208

Printed in the United States of America   10  9  8  7  6  5  4  3  2  1

First Edition

RANDOM HOUSE and colophon and LANDMARK BOOKS and colophon
are registered trademarks of Random House, Inc.

Picture credits are found on page 121.

MAR 2 4 2004

3 9082 09308 0276

*For my daughter Bethany,
who donned her first pair of combat
boots at the tender age of seventeen—and her
patriots-in-arms: Emmy Sweers, Cathy
Jeremiah, Wendy Kostinko, Jen Lackey,
Nicole Pamintuan, and Laurissa Cornish.
Thank you for serving our country.
—S.R.R.*

*ACKNOWLEDGMENTS*

I'd like to acknowledge all those individuals who so generously gave of their time and expertise to make this book as accurate and interesting as possible: Dr. Carol Berkin, Professor of History, Baruch College, City University of New York; Dr. Cynthia Kasee, Ph.D. (American Indian Studies), Interdisciplinary Studies Program, University of South Florida; Leabeth Miller, Assistant Director/Collections Manager, Oneida Nation Museum, Oneida, Wisconsin; Tom Mooney, Archivist, Cherokee Heritage Center, Park Hill, Oklahoma; Caren Knoyer, Marketing Director at Oglebay Resort and Conference Center, and Holly McCluskey, Director of Museums of Oglebay Institute, Wheeling, West Virginia; Michele Hayslett, with Information Services at the State Library of North Carolina; the knowledgeable staff at Guilford Courthouse National Military Park in North Carolina; the many faceless and often nameless historical society volunteers who answered my e-mail inquiries; the friendly librarians at Mesa Public Library in Los Alamos, New Mexico, who never cringe at my endless stream of interlibrary loan requests; my agent, Irene Kraas, who is still waiting patiently for that "adult novel"; my friend Jennifer McKerley, who good-naturedly put up with my whining about writing dilemmas; and last but certainly not least, I'd like to thank Shana Corey, my indefatigable editor, and her able assistant, Angela Roberts, who spent long hours hunting for just the right period art to bring this book to life.

# CONTENTS

# PATRIOTS IN PETTICOATS

## HEROINES OF THE
## AMERICAN REVOLUTION

THE ORIGINAL THIRTEEN COLONIES

District of Maine in Massachusetts

New Hampshire

New York

Massachusetts

Connecticut

Rhode Island

Pennsylvania

New Jersey

Maryland

Delaware

Virginia

North Carolina

South Carolina

Georgia

## MASSACHUSETTS
1. Deborah Samson
2. Mercy Otis Warren
3. Phillis Wheatley
4. Prudence Cummings Wright

## NEW YORK
5. Margaret Cochran Corbin
6. Sybil Ludington

## NEW JERSEY
7. Mary Hays
8. Rebecca Stillwell Willets

## PENNSYLVANIA
9. Sarah Franklin Bache
10. Polly Cooper
11. Lydia Darragh
12. Esther Reed
13. Betsy Ross

## MARYLAND
14. Mary Katharine Goddard

## FRONTIER (NOW WEST VIRGINIA)
15. "Mad" Ann Trotter Bailey
16. Elizabeth "Betty" Zane

## NORTH CAROLINA
17. Martha Bell
18. Kerenhappuch Turner
19. Nancy Ward

## SOUTH CAROLINA
20. Emily Geiger
21. Elizabeth Hutchinson Jackson
22. Dicey Langston

## GEORGIA
23. Nancy Morgan Hart
24. Mammy Kate

# DAUGHTERS OF LIBERTY

In 1773, America was not yet a country. It was made up of thirteen colonies. These colonies were Connecticut, Delaware, Georgia, Maryland, Massachusetts, New Hampshire, New Jersey, New York, North Carolina, Pennsylvania, Rhode Island, South Carolina, and Virginia.

Great Britain ruled these colonies. Great Britain was the world's most powerful nation. It had colonies all over the world.

Angry colonists gather to read the Stamp Act, one of the taxes passed by Great Britain. The Stamp Act forced the colonists to pay a tax on every printed document, even playing cards!

But many of the colonists in North America were not happy. They did not want to obey the laws of Great Britain because they did not get to help make those laws. They did not want to pay taxes to Great Britain either. They were already paying colony taxes.

When the British government did not listen to their complaints, the people in the thirteen colonies rebelled against King George and the British Empire. A long war followed. This is known as the *American Revolution*.

Those who wanted to become independent Americans were called *rebels* or *Whigs*. The colonists who remained loyal to the king were called *loyalists* and sometimes *Tories*.

★ ★ ★ ★

# STICKS AND STONES

Angry colonists had many bad names for the British and their supporters. They called British soldiers *redcoats* or *lobsterbacks* because of their red uniforms. Any American colonist who remained loyal to the British king was called a *Tory*. This was a serious insult. As the war dragged on, the word *Tory* came to mean "traitor."

There were many brave rebels during the American Revolution. George Washington, Paul Revere, Thomas Jefferson, and John Paul Jones are just a few. Today, these men are called *patriots*. A patriot is someone who loves and defends his or her country.

There were many women patriots during the American Revolution too. This book is about those women—the patriots who wore petticoats!

★ ★ ★ ★

# WHAT IS A PETTICOAT?

A petticoat, or pettiskirt, is a woman's long slip or undergarment. It is worn under a long dress. Some petticoats are beautifully trimmed with ruffles or embroidery. They can be made from polished cotton, satin, or silk.

During the war years, American women stopped wearing petticoats

Some of the petticoat patriots were farm girls. Some were frontier women. Others were the daughters of rich merchants or the mistresses of large farms. Many were married to soldiers. Still others were the mothers of soldiers in Washington's army.

Many of the women called themselves "Daughters of Liberty." Even before the war began, they wanted to show their support for America's "Liberty Boys."

that were made in England or were fashioned from fine British cloth. Instead, colonial women wore simple petticoats they made themselves from home-spun wool.

The women planned successful boycotts. That means they would not buy or use British goods that were taxed. These women refused to drink tea shipped from England. They refused to buy English cloth too. When this happened, the British merchants lost money. They became angry with American women. But the boycotts worked. Many unfair laws were changed.

Many women patriots wore special red, white, and blue pins and ribbons. Some even wore buckles on their shoes that were shaped like colonial flags. The women did this right under the noses of the British soldiers.

When the war began, the Daughters of Liberty eagerly took part in America's fight for freedom.

Some women went door to door collecting money. They used the money to buy medicine, boots, and gunpowder for the patriot army.

The colonies did not have stores like ours today. Women made almost everything by hand. This engraving shows women cooking over a fire, spinning yarn, churning butter, and kneading dough.

In some towns, women started spinning societies to spin wool for uniforms. They sewed quilts and dipped candles for the soldiers to use. They held meetings to discuss liberty and equality under the law.

The British and the loyalists made fun of these women. They called them "George Washington's Sewing Circle."

When the men went off to fight, the women were left alone to run the farms and businesses. They had to plant and harvest the crops by themselves. It was important to raise food for themselves and the army.

THE
Country Houfewife
AND
LADY's DIRECTO
IN THE
Management of a House, and
Delights and Profits of a Farm
CONTAINING
Instructions for managing the B
Houfe, and Malt Liquors in the Cellar;
making of Wines of all forts.
Directions for the Dairy, in the Improve
of Butter and Cheefe upon the worft of S
the feeding and making of Brawn; the ord
of Fish, Fowl, Herbs, Roots, and all othe
ful Branches belonging to a Country Seat, i
moft elegant manner for the Table.
Practical Observations concerning Distill
with the beft Method of making Ketchup, and
other curious and durable Sauces.
The whole diftributed in their proper Months, fr
Beginning to the End of the Year.
With particular Remarks relating to the Drying or Kiln
SAFFRON.

By R. BRADLEY,
Profeffor of Botany in the Univerfity of Cambr
and F. R. S.

The Sixth Edition.
With Additions.

LONDON:
Printed for D. Browne, at the Black-Swan without Temp
MDCCXXXVI.
[Price 2s. 6d.]

Many women brought this popular book with them when they left Great Britain to move to the colonies. It taught them how to grow and preserve vegetables, how to prepare meats, how to brew beer and ale, and other important skills they needed to run a household.

The women operated the flour and lumber mills. They ran butcher shops and newspaper offices. They were in charge of bakeries and fish markets.

Many women even went to war with their husbands. They made themselves useful on and off the battlefield. They brewed medicines and rolled bandages. They cooked food and washed laundry. They carried water for the soldiers. Some women actually fought in battles. Others risked their lives to deliver secret messages.

During the war, American women found many ways to serve their new country. These petticoat patriots played an important role in the birth of our nation.

# ★ 2 ★
# PATRIOTS WITH PEN AND INK

At the time of the American Revolution, there were no computers or televisions. The colonists read the latest news in pamphlets and newspapers. Many Americans wrote long letters to faraway friends and relatives, telling about events in their towns. Everyone was eager to hear what was going on in the other colonies. When the war started, women quickly learned to use their pens to help the cause. They used words to encourage the patriots. They also used words to injure the enemy.

**Phillis Wheatley** came from Africa on a
slave ship in 1761. She was purchased by
Mr. and Mrs. John Wheatley, a kind
Quaker couple who lived in Boston,
Massachusetts. The Wheatleys raised the
little girl as their own daughter.

1753–
1784

11

At first, Phillis could not speak English. But she was a quick learner. In fact, she was such a bright child that the Wheatleys hired special teachers to give Phillis the very best education. The Wheatleys also gave Phillis her freedom.

Young Phillis liked to write poetry. In 1773, she became the first African American ever to publish a book of poems.

This is the title page from Phillis Wheatley's collection of poems. After her book was published, she visited London, England. English nobles, who were against slavery, treated her like a celebrity!

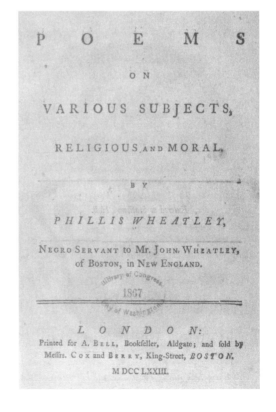

P O E M S

O N

VARIOUS SUBJECTS,

RELIGIOUS AND MORAL.

B Y

PHILLIS WHEATLEY,

NEGRO SERVANT to Mr. JOHN WHEATLEY, of BOSTON, in NEW ENGLAND.

1867

LONDON:

Printed for A. BELL, Bookseller, Aldgate; and sold by Messrs. COX and BERRY, King-Street, BOSTON.

M DCC LXXIII.

The title of the book was *Poems on Various Subjects, Religious and Moral.* Many of the poems were about the evils of slavery.

Phillis wrote poetry about liberty and freedom. She also wrote a poem titled "To His Excellency General Washington." In this poem, she praised George Washington and urged him to carry on America's fight for freedom. She wrote:

*Proceed, great chief, with virtue on*
*thy side,*
*Thy ev'ry action let the goddess guide.*
*A crown, a mansion, and a throne*
*that shine,*
*With gold unfading, WASHINGTON!*
*be thine.*

Washington was so pleased by the poem that he invited Miss Wheatley to have tea with him at his Continental Army camp!

**Mercy Otis Warren** had five sons and a
farm to take care of. But she still found
time to write angry letters to newspapers
in Massachusetts.

In 1765, she wrote about her dislike

1728–
1814

of the British king. She could not sign her name to these letters. If she did, the British would have hanged her for betraying her country. This is called *treason.*

Mercy also wrote plays. These were published as pamphlets. Sometimes, Mercy invited other patriots to her home to act them out. The British and their allies were always the villains and the clowns in Mercy's plays.

One of her plays was called *The Block-heads.* In it, Mercy made fun of the British and their loyalist friends.

Patriots like Samuel Adams and John Hancock thought the play was very funny. The British officials did not! But what could they do? They did not know who wrote the play. Mercy had not signed her name to it.

*A Model Celebration* was another of Mercy's popular plays. This comedy had mermaids and other sea creatures enjoying the fine British tea that had been dumped in

Boston Harbor at the famous Boston Tea Party in 1773.

After the war began, Mercy wrote letters encouraging all Americans to fight. One letter said:

*And be it known to Britain . . . that even American daughters are politicians and*

# TIME FOR TEA!

The Boston Tea Party was a protest by American colonists against the British tax on imported tea. In the winter of 1773, British ships, loaded with tea, arrived in Boston Harbor. On the night of December 16, several men, dressed as Indians, boarded the ships and threw the crates of tea overboard!

In October 1774, almost a year after the Boston Tea Party, Penelope Barker

*patriots and will aid the good work with their female efforts.*

Mercy also wrote to important leaders such as Thomas Jefferson and Benjamin Franklin. She wanted to share her ideas about a new American government with them.

These men often wrote back to her.

of Edenton, North Carolina, hosted another kind of tea party. She invited more than fifty female friends. She asked them to sign a statement declaring that they would not buy British tea or cloth.

Unlike the men in Boston who dressed up as Indians, the ladies of Edenton boldly signed their names so everyone would know they supported the patriot cause.

They urged her to keep writing letters to the newspapers. Her powerful way with words kept Americans fighting for liberty. It is no wonder that the rebels nicknamed Mercy the "Penwoman of the Cause."

## Mary Katharine Goddard and her

1738–1816

brother owned the first newspaper in Baltimore, Maryland. It was called the *Maryland Journal*. Mary Kate was a good editor and a good patriot too. When her brother left the newspaper business, she became the new publisher and owner of the paper.

On April 19, 1775, the first shot of the Revolution was fired at the Battle of Lexington and Concord. This shot was called "the shot heard around the world."

Mary Kate knew that it was important to write quickly and accurately about the Revolution. Relying on eyewitness reports, letters, and news sheets from other towns, she wrote about the battle. Then she printed and sold the newspaper on the same day she received her information. Soon everyone was reading Mary Kate's paper for the latest war news.

On July 4, 1776, fifty-six courageous men met in Philadelphia and agreed to sign the Declaration of Independence. In this important document, Americans declared their freedom from Britain and the king. The signers understood that if they lost the war, they would be shot or hanged as traitors.

By August, all the patriot leaders had signed the Declaration. But the printers in Philadelphia would not print the dangerous document. After all, King George might consider *that* an act of treason too.

In December 1776, the British marched into Philadelphia. The patriot leaders fled to Baltimore and assembled there. They brought with them a few handwritten copies of the Declaration of Independence.

When the secretary of the Congress asked Mary Katharine Goddard to print copies of the Declaration, she bravely agreed to do so.

She set the type and ran the presses. She proudly printed her own name at the bottom of the copies as the official printer.

Once the copies were made, the new government realized that it did not have enough money to pay to have the documents delivered throughout the colonies. What could it do?

Again, the Baltimore patriot came to its aid. Using her own money, Mary Kate paid the post riders to deliver the Declaration of Independence throughout the brand-new United States of America.

In colonial days, post riders carried the mail (then called "the post") on horseback from town to town. This post rider blows a horn to announce his arrival.

# In CONGRESS, July 4, 1776.

## THE UNANIMOUS

# DECLARATION

### OF THE

## THIRTEEN UNITED STATES OF AMERICA.

WHEN, in the Course of human Events, it becomes neceſſary for one People to diſſolve the Political Bands which have connected them with another, and to aſſume, among the Powers of the Earth, the ſeparate and equal Station to which the Laws of Nature and of Nature's GOD entitle them, a decent Reſpect to the Opinions of Mankind requires that they ſhould declare the Cauſes which impel them to the Separation.

We hold theſe Truths to be ſelf-evident, that all Men are created equal, that they are endowed, by their CREATOR, with certain unalienable Rights, that among theſe are Life, Liberty, and the Purſuit of Happineſs.—That to ſecure theſe Rights, Governments are inſtituted among Men, deriving their juſt Powers from the Conſent of the Governed, that whenever any Form of Government becomes deſtructive of theſe Ends, it is the Right of the People to alter or to aboliſh it, and to inſtitute new Government, laying its Foundation on ſuch Principles, and organizing its Powers in ſuch Form, as to them ſhall ſeem moſt likely to effect their Safety and Happineſs. Prudence, indeed, will dictate, that Governments long eſtabliſhed, ſhould not be changed for light and tranſient Cauſes; and accordingly all Experience hath ſhewn, that Mankind are more diſpoſed to ſuffer, while Evils are ſufferable, than to right themſelves by aboliſhing the Forms to which they are accuſtomed. But when a long Train of Abuſes and Uſurpations, purſuing invariably the ſame Object, evinces a Deſign to reduce them under abſolute Deſpotiſm, it is their Right, it is their Duty, to throw off ſuch Government, and to provide new Guards for their future Security. Such has been the patient Sufferance of theſe Colonies; and ſuch is now the Neceſſity which conſtrains them to alter their former Syſtems of Government. The Hiſtory of the preſent King of Great-Britain is a Hiſtory of repeated Injuries and Uſurpations, all having in direct Object the Eſtabliſhment of an abſolute Tyranny over theſe States. To prove this, let Facts be ſubmitted to a candid World.

He has refuſed his Aſſent to Laws, the moſt wholeſome and neceſſary for the public Good.

He has forbidden his Governors to paſs Laws of immediate and preſſing Importance, unleſs ſuſpended in their Operation till his Aſſent ſhould be obtained; and when ſo ſuſpended, he has utterly neglected to attend to them.

He has refuſed to paſs other Laws for the Accommodation of large Diſtricts of People, unleſs thoſe People would relinquiſh the Right of Repreſentation in the Legiſlature, a Right ineſtimable to them, and formidable to Tyrants only.

He has called together Legiſlative Bodies at Places unuſual, uncomfortable, and diſtant from the Depoſitory of their public Records, for the ſole Purpoſe of fatiguing them into Compliance with his Meaſures.

He has diſſolved Repreſentative Houſes repeatedly, for oppoſing with manly Firmneſs Invaſions on the Rights of the People.

He has refuſed for a long Time, after ſuch Diſſolutions, to cauſe others to be elected; whereby the Legiſlative Powers, incapable of Annihilation, have returned to the People at large for their exerciſe; the State remaining in the mean Time expoſed to all the Dangers of Invaſion from without, and Convulſions within.

He has endeavoured to prevent the Population of theſe States; for that Purpoſe obſtructing the Laws for Naturalization of Foreigners; refuſing to paſs others to encourage their Migration hither, and raiſing the Conditions of new Appropriations of Lands.

He has obſtructed the Adminiſtration of Juſtice, by refuſing his Aſſent to Laws for eſtabliſhing Judiciary Powers.

He has made Judges dependent on his Will alone, for the Tenure of their Offices, and the Amount and Payment of their Salaries.

He has erected a Multitude of new Offices, and ſent hither Swarms of Officers to harraſs our People, and eat out their Subſtance.

He has kept among us, in Times of Peace, Standing Armies, without the Conſent of our Legiſlatures.

He has affected to render the Military independent of and ſuperior to the Civil Power.

He has combined with others to ſubject us to a Juriſdiction foreign to our Conſtitution, and unacknowledged by our Laws; giving his Aſſent to their Acts of pretended Legiſlation:

For quartering large Bodies of Armed Troops among us:

For protecting them, by a mock Trial, from Puniſhment for any Murders which they ſhould commit on the Inhabitants of theſe States:

For cutting off our Trade with all Parts of the World:

For impoſing Taxes on us without our Conſent:

For depriving us, in many Caſes, of the Benefits of Trial by Jury:

For tranſporting us beyond Seas to be tried for pretended Offences:

For aboliſhing the free Syſtem of Engliſh Laws in a neighbouring Province, eſtabliſhing therein an arbitrary Government, and enlarging its Boundaries, ſo as to render it at once an Example and fit Inſtrument for introducing the ſame abſolute Rule into theſe Colonies:

For taking away our Charters, aboliſhing our moſt valuable Laws, and altering fundamentally the Forms of our Governments:

For ſuſpending our own Legiſlatures, and declaring themſelves inveſted with Power to legiſlate for us in all Caſes whatſoever.

He has abdicated Government here, by declaring us out of his Protection, and waging War againſt us.

He has plundered our Seas, ravaged our Coaſts, burnt our Towns, and deſtroyed the Lives of our People.

He is, at this Time, tranſporting large Armies of foreign Mercenaries to complete the Works of Death, Deſolation, and Tyranny, already begun with Circumſtances of Cruelty and Perfidy, ſcarcely paralleled in the moſt barbarous Ages, and totally unworthy the Head of a civilized Nation.

He has conſtrained our Fellow-Citizens, taken Captive on the high Seas, to bear Arms againſt their Country, to become the Executioners of their Friends and Brethren, or to fall themſelves by their Hands.

He has excited domeſtic Inſurrections amongſt us, and has endeavoured to bring on the Inhabitants of our Frontiers, the merciless Indian Savages, whoſe known Rule of Warfare, is an undiſtinguiſhed Deſtruction, of all Ages, Sexes, and Conditions.

In every Stage of theſe Oppreſſions we have Petitioned for Redreſs in the moſt humble Terms: Our repeated Petitions have been anſwered only by repeated Injury. A Prince, whoſe Character is thus marked by every Act which may define a Tyrant, is unfit to be the Ruler of a free People.

Nor have we been wanting in Attentions to our Britiſh Brethren. We have warned them, from Time to Time, of Attempts by their Legiſlature to extend an unwarrantable Juriſdiction over us. We have reminded them of the Circumſtances of our Emigration and Settlement here. We have appealed to their native Juſtice and Magnanimity, and we have conjured them by the Ties of our common Kindred to diſavow theſe Uſurpations, which would inevitably interrupt our Connections and Correſpondence. They too have been deaf to the Voice of Juſtice and of Conſanguinity. We muſt, therefore, acquieſce in the Neceſſity, which denounces our Separation, and hold them, as we hold the reſt of Mankind, Enemies in War, in Peace, Friends.

We, therefore, the Repreſentatives of the UNITED STATES OF AMERICA, in General Congreſs, Aſſembled, appealing to the Supreme Judge of the World for the Rectitude of our Intentions, do, in the Name, and by Authority of the good People of theſe Colonies, ſolemnly Publiſh and Declare, That theſe United Colonies are, and of Right ought to be, FREE AND INDEPENDENT STATES; that they are abſolved from all Allegiance to the Britiſh Crown, and that all political Connexion between them and the State of Great-Britain, is, and ought to be, totally diſſolved; and that as FREE AND INDEPENDENT STATES, they have full Power to levy War, conclude Peace, contract Alliances, eſtabliſh Commerce, and to do all other Acts and Things which INDEPENDENT STATES may of Right do. And for the Support of this Declaration, with a firm Reliance on the Protection of DIVINE PROVIDENCE, we mutually pledge to each other our Lives, our Fortunes, and our ſacred Honour.

## John Hancock.

| | | | | | |
|---|---|---|---|---|---|
| GEORGIA, | Button Gwinnett, Lyman Hall, Geo. Walton. | DELAWARE, | Cæſar Rodney, Geo. Read. | MASSACHUSETTS-BAY. | Saml. Adams, John Adams, Robt. Treat Paine, Elbridge Gerry. |
| NORTH-CAROLINA, | Wm. Hooper, Joſeph Hewes, John Penn. | VIRGINIA, { George Wythe, Richard Henry Lee, Benjn. Harriſon, Thos. Nelſon, jr. Francis Lightfoot Lee, Carter Braxton. | NEW-YORK, | Wm. Floyd, Phil. Livingſton, Frans. Lewis, Lewis Morris. | RHODE-ISLAND AND PROVIDENCE, &c. | Step. Hopkins, William Ellery. |
| SOUTH-CAROLINA, | Edward Rutledge, Thos. Heyward, junr. Thomas Lynch, junr. Arthur Middleton. | PENNSYLVANIA, { Robt. Morris, Benjamin Ruſh, Benja. Franklin, John Morton, Geo. Clymer, Jas. Smith, Geo. Taylor, James Wilſon, Geo. Roſs. | NEW-JERSEY, | Richd. Stockton, Jno. Witherſpoon, Fras. Hopkinſon, John Hart, Abra. Clark. | CONNECTICUT, | Roger Sherman, Saml. Huntington, Wm. Williams, Oliver Wolcott. |
| MARYLAND, | Samuel Chaſe, Wm. Paca, Thos. Stone, Charles Carroll, of Carrollton. | | | NEW-HAMPSHIRE, | Joſiah Bartlett, Wm. Whipple, Matthew Thornton. |

## In CONGRESS, January 18, 1777.

ORDERED,

THAT an authenticated Copy of the DECLARATION of INDEPENDENCY, with the Names of the MEMBERS of CONGRESS, ſubſcribing the ſame, be ſent to each of the UNITED STATES, and that they be deſired to have the ſame put on RECORD.

By Order of CONGRESS,

## JOHN HANCOCK, Preſident.

BALTIMORE, In MARYLAND: Printed by MARY KATHARINE GODDARD.

# ★ 3 ★
# THE NEEDLEWORKERS

In colonial times, most women knew how to sew and knit. They put these important skills to good use during the war years.

The soldiers needed thousands of sweaters and scarves, especially during the cold winters. The new colonial government did not have enough money to buy uniforms for all the men.

American women throughout the colonies formed sewing circles to make quilts and knit socks for the cause. Even Martha

## LIBERTY SPINNING BEES

Homespun cloth became very important during the war when the colonists refused to buy English cloth. American women did all the spinning and weaving of home-spun. This was quite a chore, but the Daughters of Liberty turned it into something social by hosting parties called "spinning bees."

Sometimes, they held contests to see who could spin the most wool.

Washington, the wife of America's most famous general, woke up early each morning to knit socks. Many times she visited General Washington's army camp. She brought food and blankets. She stayed up late each night mending clothes for the soldiers. Other women helped provide the army with clothing too.

In his diary, the colonist Ezra Stiles wrote about a spinning bee held at his house in 1769. He guessed that about six hundred guests showed up to spin or to watch the spinners. Everyone brought food. Some brought musical instruments to entertain the women at the spinning wheels.

**Esther Reed** of Pennsylvania was the
mother of five small children. She was also
a patriot. Esther wanted to do something
special to help the brave men in Washington's army. She decided to start a
fund drive to raise money so that every
soldier could have a salary bonus.

1746–
1780

She wrote to General Washington to tell him of her plan. But Washington had another idea. He told her that his soldiers needed new uniforms more than money. He suggested that the women of Philadelphia make clothes for his men.

Here is part of George Washington's letter to Esther Reed. He says, "The patriotism of the Ladies entitles them to the highest applause of this Country.... I would propose the purchasing of coarse Linen, to be made into Shirts, with the whole amount of their subscription."

So Esther began collecting money from her neighbors to buy cloth and thread to make thousands of shirts for George Washington's soldiers. Unfortunately, Esther Reed became very ill. She died before her project was

---

★ ★ ★ ★

# WHAT IS A SAMPLER?

There were no sewing machines during the American Revolution. There were no clothing stores either. Learning to sew was very important, and girls during the colonial period spent more than an hour a day practicing their stitches. They embroidered pretty designs or common sayings, such as "Home Sweet Home," on pieces of cloth.

These were called "samplers." They provided "samples" of a girl's handiwork. The samplers were framed and hung on the walls of the girls' homes.

completed. What would happen? Who would see that all the shirts were finished? Who would deliver them to General Washington? Luckily, another patriot in petticoats came to the rescue.

This sampler was made in 1792 by Patty Coggeshall of Rhode Island when she was just twelve years old!

**Sarah Franklin Bache** lived in Philadelphia with her husband and young children. Sarah was also the daughter of the patriot Benjamin Franklin.

1743– 1808

Sarah knew how important Esther's project was. When Esther died, Sarah offered to take over.

She continued to collect money. She organized sewing groups. She even asked the women who made the shirts to sew their names in the collars. This made the shirts extra special for Washington's grateful soldiers. They knew that American women had made the shirts with care and that the women had been proud to sew their names inside.

Esther Reed and Sarah Franklin Bache were leaders of the Ladies Association of Philadelphia. The group is shown here in 1780, gathered to sew shirts for General Washington's Continental Army.

**Betsy Ross** is the most famous patriot

1752–
1836

with a needle. When she was a girl, she learned to make sofas and chair pillows. She learned to sew flags too.

When she grew up, she and her husband, John, started their own upholstering business. They worked very hard. They went to church on Sundays. Sometimes, General George Washington sat in the pew across from them.

When John joined the Pennsylvania militia, Betsy ran the business by herself. There were not many customers because people gave much of their money to the war effort.

In 1776, John was wounded in an explosion. The army sent him home to recover. Betsy did all she could to make him well again. But John Ross died. Betsy was a widow.

According to legend, George Washington and two of his friends came to see

It is said that George Washington originally thought the stars on the flag should have six points, but Betsy Ross showed him how she could cut out a star with five points with just one snip of her scissors!

Betsy. They told her how important it was that the new nation have a flag of its own. They handed her a picture of the flag they wanted her to sew. It had red and white stripes. There was also a blue field in the corner with a circle of thirteen white stars—one for each colony.

Did Betsy Ross *really* make the first Stars and Stripes? There are no facts to prove the story is true. But we *do* know that Betsy sewed many flags during the war. Every fort wanted a flag. Each army troop wanted a flag too. At that time, there were no official standards for state and military flags like there are today. So not all flags looked the same.

Regardless of whether Betsy Ross really sewed the *first* Old Glory, there are government records that show she was paid by the State Navy Board of Pennsylvania to make flags for navy ships. She *was* a patriot who served America with her needle.

Betsy Ross's house still stands today. If you visit Philadelphia, you can take a tour and learn more about Betsy Ross.

# ★ 4 ★
# NOBLE NURSES

Many women during the American Revolution served their country by taking care of the sick and injured. This was not easy. There were not enough bandages to keep wounded men clean. There was not enough food to keep them well fed. Smallpox and other diseases killed many people during the war years. Even the caregivers sometimes fell ill and died.

General George Washington asked Congress to hire army nurses to care for the sick and wounded soldiers. Congress did so.

The nurses were paid two dollars a month. By 1777, army nurses were so important to the war effort that Congress raised their wages to eight dollars per month. But not all nurses worked for pay. Some women volunteered to be nurses.

**Elizabeth Hutchinson Jackson** traveled more than a hundred miles from her home on the border of North and South Carolina to reach Charleston Harbor. The British held two of her sons captive on a prison ship there. Andrew, her youngest son, was only thirteen years old.

1740?–1781

Elizabeth Hutchinson Jackson gave birth to one of her sons, Andrew Jackson, in this North Carolina log cabin in 1767.

Elizabeth received permission to take care of her sons. Both were sick with smallpox. Most of the other rebel prisoners were also sick or wounded. There were no doctors or nurses to care for the sick men. The food was bad, and the water was unclean.

Elizabeth took pity on the men. She made soup for them. She cleaned their wounds and changed their bandages. She

While in prison, thirteen-year-old Andrew Jackson refused to polish the boots of a British officer. As punishment, the officer struck the young boy's forehead with a sword. Andrew had a scar from this for the rest of his life.

worked all day and late into the night for many weeks.

When her older son Robert died, Elizabeth begged the British officers to release young Andrew. They finally agreed, and she sent the boy home. But she didn't go with him. She stayed in Charleston to take care of the other dying prisoners.

After many months, Elizabeth caught a fever. She died in Charleston in 1781.

Her teenage son Andrew was now an orphan. He kept fighting the British troops. He always blamed the British for the death of his mother.

When Andrew Jackson grew up, he became the seventh president of the United States.

This is an engraved portrait of Andrew Jackson, made around the time he was the president of the United States. It was engraved by J. B. Longacre.

# Kerenhappuch Turner (keh-run-HAP-

pick) was born in the colony of Virginia. She was in her eighties when she
received news that her grown son
had been wounded in a battle with
British troops.

Unknown—
1805

Kerenhappuch knew that there
were not many doctors to take care of
wounded soldiers. Medicine was hard to
find. Soldiers often died. She decided
that her son would have a better chance
to get well if she took care of him herself.

Despite her age, she made the long
journey to the North Carolina battlefield
on horseback. She took clean bandages
and medicine with her.

Kerenhappuch found her son just in
time. He was almost dead. His leg was so
damaged that the army doctor wanted to
cut it off.

But Kerenhappuch promised to take
care of her son and his wounded leg. She

stayed for many weeks. She gently cleaned her son's wound over and over again. Kerenhappuch took care of other wounded soldiers too. When she finally returned home, she took her son with her. He limped, but he walked on his own two legs!

Today, you can see a statue of this amazing nurse at the Guilford Courthouse National Military Park in North Carolina.

This statue of Kerenhappuch Turner, put up on July 4, 1902, is believed to be the first ever to honor a heroine of the Revolutionary War.

**Polly Cooper** was an Oneida (o-NYE-duh) woman. While neighboring tribes fought for the British, the Oneida sided with the colonists in the war. They played an important part in the American victory at the Battle of Saratoga in 1777.

Dates Unknown

Polly and other Oneida also traveled from New York to Pennsylvania to see George Washington. They delivered corn to his starving soldiers during the hard winter months at Valley Forge in 1777 and 1778.

Life at Valley Forge was very hard. There was little food. This picture shows Washington visiting a wounded soldier. Other soldiers are gathered around a fire to keep warm.

When Polly saw the sick and suffering men, she decided to stay with Washington's army. She went right to work. She cooked wholesome soups for the sick soldiers. She made special medicines for the wounded ones.

During battles, Polly took water to the thirsty fighting men. She even cooked hot, hearty meals for General Washington and his staff.

George Washington offered to pay Polly for her hard work. But she refused to accept the money. Washington wanted to thank Polly for her kindness to his men. Martha Washington suggested he give her a present. It was a beautiful black shawl.

Polly kept it all of her life. Today, Polly Cooper's shawl is still owned by members of the Oneida tribe. It is an important historic relic. It is a symbol of George Washington's gratitude for Polly's service to our country.

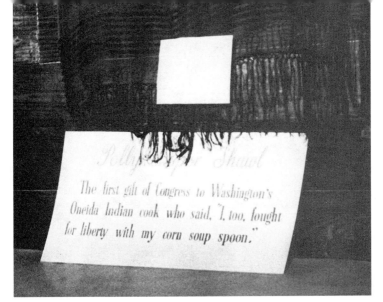

The first gift of Congress to Washington's Oneida Indian cook who said, "I, too, fought for liberty with my corn soup spoon."

Polly Cooper's shawl is owned by one of her descendants.

★ ★ ★ ★

# THE WORM THAT SAVES LIVES!

Did you know that doctors in the colonial period often used a special kind of worm to help them cure sick patients?

These worms are called *leeches*. They suck the blood of humans. When the leech is full, it pops off. Doctors called this "bleeding" a patient. They thought some people got sick because they had "bad blood."

# ★ 5 ★
# DARING DEFENDERS

From the very beginning of the war with England, American women proved to be brave and strong. They were bold and clever too. Because they loved their homes, families, and communities, they were willing to take risks to protect them. With the men gone off to war, women were left alone to defend the home front. They confronted the enemy—sometimes right on their own front steps.

**Nancy Morgan Hart** was a gutsy frontier patriot from Georgia. She was tall and had bright red hair and blue eyes. The Indians there called her "War Woman" because she fought so bravely against the British army and their loyalist supporters.

1735?–1830

✶ ✶ ✶ ✶

# LET'S TALK TURKEY!

If Benjamin Franklin had had his way, the wild turkey would have been our country's symbol, not the bald eagle.

Franklin served on a committee to select an official seal for the new nation. The bald eagle was the popular choice. But Franklin was not shy about voicing his objections. He wrote:

*The bald eagle . . . is a bird of bad moral character . . . he is therefore*

There are many exciting tales about Nancy's bravery. One tells of the day six loyalist soldiers invaded Nancy's cabin. Her husband was not at home. The soldiers killed her last turkey and ordered her to cook it.

Nancy knew these men were dangerous.

*by no means a proper emblem for the brave and honest . . . America.*

*. . . The turkey is in comparison a much more respectable bird . . . and would not hesitate to attack a grenadier of the British guards, who should presume to invade his farmyard with a red coat on.*

They had killed a popular colonial officer while he was sleeping at home in his bed.

Nancy cooked the turkey. Legend tells us that she then quietly sent one of her young daughters to the well to summon Mr. Hart by blowing on a conch shell.

Then Nancy gave the men some whiskey. When they were drunk, she began slipping their muskets through a chink in the cabin wall. She wanted her husband and daughter to have weapons to fight with when they arrived.

Caught in the act, Nancy grabbed a musket. She shot one of the men. She wounded another when he tried to take the gun away from her.

When Nancy's husband, Benjamin, arrived with his friends, they were probably surprised. The soldiers stood in a corner of the cabin with their arms over their heads. Nancy had taken them captive all by herself!

Today, there is a highway and a state park in Georgia named for Nancy Hart.

**Rebecca Stillwell Willets** saved her small New Jersey town from the redcoats.

1750– Unknown

All the men and boys who were at least fifteen years old were away, fighting in the Continental Army. Only women and children were left in Beesley's Point.

The town had a ferry house near the shore to store ropes and other ferryboat equipment. But it was also filled with food and clothing and supplies for Washington's army. Loyalist spies learned of the storehouse. They told the British about it. They also told the British that there were no men to defend the town.

"Easy pickings!" the British may have thought. They planned a raid.

But Rebecca was a soldier's daughter and a soldier's wife too. She watched the beach with her spyglass.

One day, she saw a British ship approach. It lowered a small boat. Many sailors climbed down into the boat. The sailors started rowing toward the beach to the ferry house.

Rebecca guessed what was going to happen. She had to protect the women and children of Beesley's Point. And she had to protect the supplies in the ferry house.

Lifting her skirts, Rebecca ran down the hill to the cannon in front of the ferry house. It was loaded and ready for action. Rebecca waited until the boat full of redcoats was in range. Then she fired the cannon. *Kaboom!*

The British sailors were surprised. They

Cannons like this one at Yorktown Battlefield in Yorktown, Virginia, were one of the most common types of weapons used during the Revolutionary War.

thought there must be some mistake! A patriot militia was camped in Beesley's Point to protect the supplies. Quickly, they returned to their ship and sailed away.

Rebecca had saved the day!

## Prudence Cummings Wright grew up

1723–
1824

in Hollis, New Hampshire. When she married, Prudence and her husband,

David, moved to the nearby town of Pepperell, Massachusetts.

David became a Minuteman when the talk of war began. On the night of April 18, 1775, Paul Revere rode through Pepperell. He shouted for the men to arm themselves. The British army was planning to attack!

David grabbed his musket. He and the other men and boys in town marched to Concord to fight. They were going to take

★ ★ ★ ★

## WHAT IS A MINUTEMAN?

The Minutemen were farmers, storekeepers, teachers, and other patriot volunteers. They promised to be ready to fight at a minute's notice to defend their towns from attacks by British soldiers.

part in the first battle of the Revolution.

But who would defend Pepperell from the British? Prudence rounded up some neighbor women and formed a women's militia.

They dressed up in their husbands' clothes. They armed themselves with muskets, pitchforks, and shovels. They stood guard on Jewett's Bridge. They did

This is Jewett's Bridge over the Nashua River in Pepperell, Massachusetts. In colonial days, it didn't have the roof or walls you see in the picture—those were added in the nineteenth century.

not want any redcoats marching over the bridge into their hometown.

Later that same day, the women got word that a man named Leonard Whiting was planning to cross the bridge at Pepperell. Whiting was a well-known loyalist from New Hampshire. He was on his way to Boston to deliver messages to the British.

When Whiting tried to cross the bridge on horseback, the women captured him. Some of them held him at gunpoint. Others poked their pitchforks at him. The rest searched through his clothing for secret letters. They found some in his boots.

Prudence's female soldiers took Whiting into town and locked him up. They kept watch all night. They did not want Whiting's friends to rescue him.

The following morning, some of the women marched Whiting into the next town.

Prudence and her small troop proudly turned their prisoner over to the Minutemen!

The colonies depended on slaves brought over from Africa. Slaves like Mammy Kate and the field hands pictured here often lived on big farms called plantations. The slaves did much of the hard work needed to run the colonists' homes and farms.

**Mammy Kate** was a slave. She lived in

Dates
Unknown

Georgia. Her owner, Stephen Heard, was a colonel in the American army.

During the Battle of Kettle Creek, the British wounded and then captured Colonel Heard. Mammy Kate made up her mind to rescue her young master.

She went to the British fort where Stephen was being held. She carried a large clothes basket and offered to do washing for the officers there. She asked if she could wash Colonel Heard's clothes too.

The soldiers told her that they were soon going to hang the rebel. But an officer gave her permission to see the injured colonel and to do his laundry.

Colonial laundry was often done in wash houses, like this one located at Mount Vernon, George Washington's home in Virginia. Note the large clothes basket, which may be similar to the one Mammy Kate used.

Mammy Kate visited the fort twice a week for several weeks. She took the dirty clothes home to wash and iron. She always carried a big clothes basket on her hip. One day, when delivering laundry, she whispered her plan to Master Stephen.

Stephen Heard was not a large man. But Mammy Kate was over six feet tall. She was strong too. She told her master to get into the clothes basket. She covered him with a pile of shirts.

Then she left the fort with the basket on her hip. The British soldiers waved good-bye to her.

When they were safely out of sight, Mammy Kate helped Stephen Heard out of the basket. She had two horses hidden in the bushes outside the fort. Together, they escaped on horseback.

Grateful that Kate had saved his life, Colonel Heard promised to set her free. He kept that promise and even gave Kate a tract of land and a small home of her own.

Mammy Kate later married and had nine children. Colonel Stephen Heard became the first governor of the state of Georgia after the war. The two remained friendly all their lives.

# ★ 6 ★
# SPIES AND MESSENGERS

It took a special kind of courage to be a spy or messenger during the war. Rebels who got caught spying were sometimes hanged as traitors. But this did not stop the brave women of colonial America. They sewed secret letters into their petticoats. They rode at night through enemy lines to deliver urgent messages.

When women ran errands in town, they took time to count the number of British soldiers. They counted guns and wagons too.

To the enemy, women with shopping baskets appeared quite harmless. But these women were really gathering information for patriot leaders.

## Martha Bell
was a rich farmer's wife

1735–
1820?

and mother of five children. She was also a patriot. In 1781, the British general Lord Cornwallis camped on her North Carolina plantation for two days.

One of the most important commanders of the British army, Cornwallis was responsible for the deaths of thousands of patriot soldiers. He moved into Martha's house and took over her mill. He even planned to grind Martha's corn crop to make corn bread for his soldiers.

Martha knew that the British had burned down the homes of other patriots. She asked Cornwallis if he was going to burn down her home.

When he said he would not do so, Martha allowed him to stay in the house. She told him that had he planned on burning it, she would have destroyed it herself so he couldn't use it!

Cornwallis soon moved on. American troops arrived shortly afterward.

The American officers asked if Martha would be willing to spy for them. They needed to know how many men Cornwallis had and if he was expecting more British soldiers to arrive.

Martha was happy to help. She even had a clever plan. She saddled her horse and rode straight to the British camp. She forced her way into General Cornwallis's tent. Then she loudly complained that his soldiers had stolen items from her home when they had camped there.

While the general questioned his men, Martha counted cannons and horses. Her sharp eyes observed the number of wounded men. The information she took back to the patriots helped them plan their next attack.

After that day, Martha continued to spy. She did this mostly at night. When loyalists or British stopped her, she lied to them. She said she was a midwife on her way to deliver a baby!

Today, there is a monument to Martha Bell. It is at the Guilford Courthouse National Military Park in North Carolina. It states that Martha was an "enthusiastic patriot" and a "revolutionary heroine."

MRS. MARTHA MCFARLANE MCGEE-BELL
1735 — 1820
LOYAL WHIG — ENTHUSIASTIC PATRIOT
REVOLUTIONARY HEROINE

WE ARE INDEBTED TO E. W. CARUTHERS
FOR THE EVENTFULL STORY OF HER LIFE.

ERECTED BY
ALEXANDER MARTIN CHAPTER, D. A. R.
HIGH POINT N. C.
1928

Historians think this portrait, painted in Pennsylvania in the late 1700s, is of Lydia Darragh.

# Lydia Darragh of Philadelphia, Pennsyl-

vania, is known as "the Brave Quakeress
Who Saved the Revolution."

1729–
1789

In September 1777, the British
army marched into Philadelphia. They
set up roadblocks outside the city.

One of the British leaders, General
Howe, even moved into the fine house

right across the street from Lydia's home and made it his headquarters. Lydia and her husband, William, were dismayed. But they were even more upset when the British general demanded to use *their* parlor for his staff meetings!

This painting of Lydia Darragh's house on Second Street in Philadelphia was done by William L. Breton in 1828.

One night, several high-ranking British officers came to Lydia's house. When she took their coats and hats, the men ordered Lydia and her husband to go to bed early and not to interrupt their meeting.

But Lydia couldn't sleep. Listening through the keyhole, she learned a dreadful secret. The British troops in Philadelphia were planning an attack on Washington's army at Whitemarsh!

Lydia flew back to her bed. She was afraid. She knew the British would punish her entire family if she revealed their military secrets.

But Lydia had to warn the patriots. Her son Charles was an officer with General Washington's army at Whitemarsh! He had disobeyed the strict Quaker teachings of his parents and joined the fight for American independence.

Lydia knew what she had to do. The next morning, she walked many long miles in the snow to deliver her secret message. She told the British patrol at the city roadblock that she was going to the mill to buy flour. She even showed them her empty flour sack.

Far outside the city, miles past the flour mill, Lydia gave the news about the

# WHAT IS A QUAKER?

*Quaker* is a slang name for a member of the Society of Friends. The founder of the society was an Englishman named George Fox. He preached that everyone should "tremble at the Word of the Lord." Many people made fun of him and his followers. They called them "quakers."

They were so badly treated that many Quakers left England and went to the American colonies. Many settled in

surprise attack to one of General Washington's officers near Whitemarsh. He was very grateful. If Washington's men lost this battle, it could mean the end of their fight for freedom.

Lydia begged the officer not to tell

Rhode Island and Pennsylvania. The Quakers wore plain, simple clothes. They were kind to the Indians. They did not believe in slavery and helped slaves escape from their owners.

During the Revolution, most Quakers did not fight. They helped the patriots in other ways, such as caring for the sick and wounded and donating food and blankets for the soldiers. Even today, Quakers do not believe in wars or fighting.

anyone who had brought the warning. She was afraid of what the British would do to her family.

At dawn on December 4, 1777, the British troops marched from Philadelphia to Whitemarsh to launch their attack. But General Washington's army was ready and waiting for them!

For three days, the British tried to find a weak spot in the patriots' line of defense. They finally gave up and went back to Philadelphia. After the battle, one British officer complained that General Washington's well-prepared army had made the British troops seem "like a parcel of fools."

They never found out that it was brave Lydia Darragh who had set them up for defeat. It was not until many years after the war that Lydia's daughter told the newspapers what her mother had done to help Washington's army.

**Emily Geiger** was only eighteen years old when she risked her life to deliver a message from the patriot general Nathanael Greene to another patriot officer, General Thomas Sumter.

Other messengers and scouts had failed to get letters from one patriot camp to another. Emily learned of the problem. Her family supported the patriot cause. Emily wanted to help too.

General Greene refused Emily's offer at first. He told her that it was too dangerous.

But Emily, the daughter of a rich farmer, had grown up in South Carolina. She knew the countryside.

General Greene finally agreed. He gave her a letter. It outlined a battle plan to defeat the British army. He told her to read it and memorize it in case it got lost on the way.

Emily did so. Then she hid the letter

71

down the front of her dress and set off. She realized she could be killed if she got caught.

Her journey took several days. Emily rode her father's best horse. She traveled on back roads and through swamps. She kept her eyes open for enemy troops.

Emily had almost reached Sumter's camp when three British scouts captured her. They took her to their camp headquarters. The commander, Lord Rawdon, accused Emily of being a rebel spy!

Emily denied it. Legend has it she told him she was on her way to visit a sick friend.

Lord Rawdon did not believe her. He ordered her to be searched.

The soldiers locked Emily in a room. They left to find a loyalist woman to undress the female spy and search for hidden letters.

What should she do? Emily pulled out the letter. She couldn't let them find it. She read the letter one more time and then tore it into tiny pieces.

Emily looked around the room. Where could she hide the pieces of paper? She would have to eat the letter, she decided. One by one, she chewed the bits of dry paper.

Suddenly, she heard the soldiers returning. She heard a woman's voice too. Emily chewed faster. She shoved the last pieces into her mouth just as the farmer's wife came into the room.

Emily covered her face with her hands. She did not want the woman to see her chewing. She threw herself facedown on the bunk in the corner of the room. She pretended to cry.

While the woman searched her, Emily swallowed the last bits of paper. The woman found nothing on Emily or in her clothing. Lord Rawdon let Emily go.

Later that same afternoon, young Emily Geiger safely reached General Sumter's patriot camp. She recited word for word the secret battle plans she had eaten!

**Nancy Ward** was a Cherokee woman who helped the patriots. Nancy's real name was Nanye'hi (nan-YUH-hee), or White Rose. But her white friends called

1738–
1822

# WOMEN OF THE CHEROKEE NATION

Women had important roles in Cherokee society. Many, like Nancy Ward, owned their own land and homes. The women passed the property down to their daughters, not their sons.

In 1776, the British traveler William Bartram stayed with the Cherokee to observe their society. He noted that the women's council was led by the most powerful, well-respected women in the

her Nancy. When her husband died in a battle with Creek Indians, Nancy took his place as a Cherokee warrior.

Nancy earned the title "Beloved Woman" and was an important leader of her people. She married again—this time to a white frontier trader named Bryan Ward. He lived with her on Cherokee land.

Cherokee Nation. The council could overrule decisions made by men. In fact, only the Cherokee women, not the warriors, could declare war. The women were considered more levelheaded than the men.

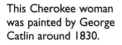

This Cherokee woman was painted by George Catlin around 1830.

When the Revolutionary War began, the Cherokee Nation took sides with the British. But not Nancy! She wanted her people to remain at peace with their colonist neighbors.

In July 1776, Nancy learned a terrible secret. A member of her tribe told her that British agents had talked the Cherokee into killing the settlers at the nearby Watauga settlement.

Nancy did not want this to happen. She warned John Sevier, the leader of the settlers at Watauga.

When the Cherokee attacked, John and his men were ready for them.

Word of Nancy's kindness spread. Soon John became an officer in the frontier militia. Nancy gave cattle and clothing to the militia.

Some Cherokee considered Nancy to be a traitor. But the settlers regarded her as a heroine.

When Sevier and his men were ordered to burn Cherokee villages, the patriots obeyed. But they did not attack Nancy Ward's village!

## "Mad" Ann Trotter Bailey was one of the most colorful heroines of the American Revolution. She was born in England. She settled in the colony of Virginia when she was nineteen.

1742–1825

Ann married a frontiersman named Richard. They built a cabin in the wilderness. She wore buckskin pants and learned to ride a horse. Richard joined the patriot army. When he was killed in battle in 1774, Ann volunteered to be a wilderness scout and messenger for the patriots.

Ann knew her way through the woods. She delivered messages from one fort to another. She spied on the British soldiers and their Shawnee allies. She talked frontier settlers into joining the patriots. Sometimes, she delivered ammunition and other supplies.

The Shawnee who fought with the British called her "Mad Ann." They thought she was crazy. She dressed like a man and carried a tomahawk. She chewed tobacco.

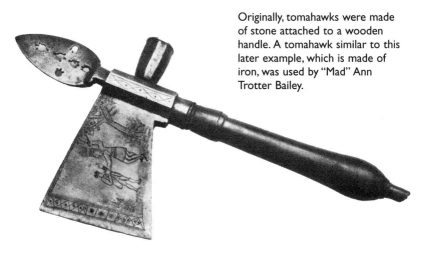

Originally, tomahawks were made of stone attached to a wooden handle. A tomahawk similar to this later example, which is made of iron, was used by "Mad" Ann Trotter Bailey.

Ann did not act like most people thought a "normal" woman acted.

Once while being chased, Ann jumped off her horse and hid inside a hollow log. The Shawnee searched everywhere but could not find her. They captured her horse and took it back to their camp.

Later that night, Ann crawled out from her hiding place. She crept into the Shawnee camp and stole back her horse. As she rode away, she laughed and let out a bloodcurdling war whoop. Mad Ann had escaped again!

Mad Ann later married an American soldier named John Bailey and lived to be a very old woman. She died in her wilderness cabin long, long after the war. There is a monument to Ann Trotter Bailey in Point Pleasant, West Virginia.

# ★ 7 ★
# SCHOOLGIRL REBELS

Not all of the American patriots were grown-ups. Some were young girls. Like their mothers and fathers, these schoolgirls loved liberty. Girls could not go to war with their brothers, so they helped in other ways. They even gave up morning school lessons to knit socks and sew homespun clothing.

In October 1775, the Connecticut teenager Betsy Foote wrote in her diary that she had "carded wool all day, then spun ten knots of wool in the evening and felt Nationaly into the bargain!" This was Betsy's way of saying she felt patriotic.

New York City teenager Charity Clarke "felt Nationaly" too when she learned to

★ ★ ★ ★

# READING, WRITING, 'RITHMETIC

During the war years, girls rarely earned more than an elementary education. It was not considered important for females to be well educated.

In the northern colonies, girls who lived in villages, towns, and cities could attend dame schools. These were run by widows or wives who needed extra money. They taught music, reading, and writing in their homes. Girls could also take classes in sewing, dancing, and fancy needlework.

knit socks for soldiers. She wrote to an English cousin and warned him that the colonies were filled with "a fighting army of amazons . . . armed with spinning wheels." She also added that "the Love of Liberty is cherished within this bosom."

In the southern colonies, rich girls were given simple lessons in reading, writing, and arithmetic by their brothers' tutors. However, the ornamental skills were considered the most important.

Young colonial girls who lived in the country often relied on family members to teach them to read and write.

# Elizabeth "Betty" Zane

Unknown–1831?

**Elizabeth "Betty" Zane** was a teenager living in what is now Wheeling, West Virginia. When the war began, Betty's family took sides against the British.

In September 1782, a large party of British soldiers and their Delaware and Shawnee allies planned to attack the American settlers near Fort Henry. When the Zane family and the other settlers heard the news, they hurried into the fort for safety.

A terrible battle began when the British attacked. The day was hot. It was filled with gun smoke and yelling and blood. The settlers were tired and thirsty. There were fewer than fifty of them to hold the fort, and the enemy numbered almost three hundred!

Betty heard the weary men talking. One of the leaders was her grown-up brother Ebenezer Zane. He mentioned that the settlers were nearly out of gunpowder.

Betty spoke up. She reminded her brother that there was plenty of gunpowder back at their cabin. She even volunteered to go get it.

The men accepted the girl's brave offer. When Betty slipped out the side entrance of the fort, the British soldiers ignored her. After all, she was only a young girl. What harm could she do? They kept shooting at the men inside the fort.

Betty rushed to her family's cabin. She bundled up the gunpowder and ran back to the fort as fast as she could. The lives of everyone inside depended on her.

This time, the redcoats *did* shoot at her. So did the Indians. They guessed that she was carrying supplies into the fort. Bullets flew all around Betty Zane!

When she reached safety, the settlers cheered. The men quickly handed out the gunpowder. They fought fiercely all night long. They put up such a good fight that the

British troops gave up early in the morning and left. This frontier battle became known as the last battle of the American Revolution.

In May 1923, the schoolchildren of West Virginia raised money to buy a statue of brave Betty Zane. They placed it near the cemetery where she is buried.

The marker reads:

IN MEMORY OF ELIZABETH ZANE
WHOSE HEROIC DEED
SAVED FORT HENRY
IN 1782

## Dicey Langston

was another daring young heroine. The fourteen-year-old lived in Laurens County, South Carolina, along with her sick

1766–1837

and elderly father, Solomon Langston.

In the summer of 1780, Dicey overheard some of her loyalist relatives talking. They were whispering about a Tory leader named "Bloody Bill" Cunningham. Cunningham and his cruel gang planned to attack a nearby patriot settlement called Little Eden.

Dicey's older brother James lived in that settlement. He was a soldier in the patriot army. He had to be warned!

Even though she did not own a horse, Dicey knew what she had to do. Leaving home in the middle of the night, she made the dangerous journey to Little Eden on foot.

Dicey tramped through marshes and crossed swollen streams in the dark. There were no bridges. Dicey feared she'd never get there in time to warn James and the other patriots of the coming attack.

Coming to the Enoree River, she threw herself into the churning, foamy waters. The current was fast. Dicey nearly drowned. She fought to keep her head above the water and allowed the river to carry her downstream.

As she neared Little Eden, Dicey pulled herself up onto the muddy bank.

Tired and wet, she stumbled to her brother's house. She blurted out the terrible news that Bloody Bill Cunningham was coming.

James rushed to warn the other patriots. He told them to flee into the marsh.

When the Tory gang attacked Little Eden the next morning, they found the settlement deserted!

Many patriot lives were saved because of Dicey's daring deed. Today, there is a monument to Dicey Langston near Travelers Rest, South Carolina.

**Sybil Ludington** is remembered as the

1761–
1839

female Paul Revere. She was sixteen years old when she played her part in American history.

Sybil lived in rural New York with her parents, Colonel and Mrs. Ludington, and her seven younger brothers and sisters. On the night of April 26, 1777, a breathless rider arrived at the Ludington home. He gasped out the news that the British were burning Danbury, Connecticut.

Colonel Ludington knew that the ammunition, grain, and molasses stored in Danbury were very important to the Continental Army. They needed these supplies to feed and arm the patriot soldiers.

The colonel agreed to round up the militia right away. But who could call his men to arms? It was late at night. He couldn't go himself. He had to gather the supplies and ammunition for his volunteer militia, and the messenger in the parlor was too worn-out to ride farther.

That's when young Sybil came to the rescue. No one knows for sure if she volunteered or if her father woke her up and asked her to go. We only know that she was brave and willing.

So the teenager and her horse, Star, raced forty miles through the dark, windy night. The roads were slippery with mud. There were deep wagon ruts in places.

Sybil rode from one farmhouse to another. She shouted for the men to wake up, fetch their guns, and meet at the Ludington home. She told them that the British were burning Danbury.

At each farmhouse, volunteer soldiers were quick to rally to Sybil's warning. Men from all over the countryside met up with Colonel Ludington. Together, they marched over ten miles to Danbury that night.

The New York volunteers arrived too

late to join the battle to save the supplies. But they did succeed in helping the Danbury patriots push the British back to their ships in Long Island Sound.

Today, there is a statue honoring daring Sybil Ludington in Carmel, New York.

This statue of Sybil Ludington was sculpted by Anna Vaughn Huntington in 1960, when Ms. Huntington was eighty-four years old!

# LADIES ON HORSEBACK

Girls and women rode sidesaddle in colonial times. It was very improper then for females to wear pants or to straddle a horse like a man.

The sidesaddle was made so women in long skirts could ride with both legs on the same side of the horse. However, it took good balance and a lot of practice for girls to keep their seat when riding this way.

## ★ 8 ★
## WOMEN ON THE BATTLEFIELD

During the American Revolution, women were not allowed to join the army. But some women and girls learned to make bullets and mend cannons at night after dinner. Others left the safety of their homes to join their husbands and fathers on the battlefields. They reloaded muskets and rifles for the fighting men. Often, they risked their lives to take fresh water and food into forts and behind battle lines. These women had unforgettable courage.

**Deborah Samson** was a young farm woman from Massachusetts. But when Deborah was twenty-one years old, she cut off her hair and pretended to be a young man. She enlisted in the Continental

1760–
1827

This image of Deborah Samson is based on a legend. The tale says that when Deborah was found to be a woman, she was told to deliver that news herself, dressed as Robert Shurtleff, in a letter to General George Washington.

Army in 1781. She said her name was Robert Shurtleff.

Deborah fought as a soldier for two years. The men teased her for being too young to shave. But they admired her pluck too. Once, she got a sword cut on the side of her head. Another time, she was shot in the shoulder. Both times, Deborah treated her own injuries.

In another battle, a bullet pierced her thigh. Her fellow patriots carried Deborah off the battlefield to the doctor's tent, even though she begged them to let her keep fighting.

Deborah would not take her trousers off in front of the doctor. She could not let anyone find out that young "Robert" was really a woman.

As soon as she was able, she crept out of the hospital tent. She used a penknife to dig the bullet out of her thigh.

One day, she came down with camp fever. This was a common sickness among the soldiers. Deborah fainted. She was carried to a camp hospital. An army doctor removed her shirt and discovered that the sick young man was really a woman!

At first, the doctor did not reveal his patient's secret. But as soon as she was well, the doctor told Deborah's commander her true identity.

Deborah was honorably discharged in 1783 and sent home. She married a farmer named Benjamin Gannett.

After the war was over, President George Washington invited Deborah to visit him. He had been told how bravely she had fought for the new nation. The Congress presented Deborah with a land grant and a soldier's pension.

In 1944, during World War II, a new Liberty ship was named *Deborah Gannett* in her honor!

# Margaret Cochran Corbin was born

on the Pennsylvania frontier.

When Margaret grew up, her husband, John, called her Molly. After John joined the Continental Army, Molly went with him. She followed John from one military camp to another.

On November 16, 1776, John Corbin manned the cannons during the fierce battle at Fort Washington in New York. Molly was right there beside him.

While John fired the cannon, Molly carried buckets of water to the thirsty men in the artillery. She also brought water to pour on the hot cannons while they were reloaded.

The soldiers teased her. They called her "Molly Pitcher" because she always had a pitcher or pail in her hands. "Molly Pitcher" was a popular nickname during the war for women who carried water to the battlefields.

When her husband was killed by enemy gunfire, the grieving Molly had no time to cry. She feared the British would win the battle. She dropped her water bucket. Then Molly reloaded the cannon. She fired the big gun, just as she'd seen John do. She did not stop until an enemy bullet wounded her in the shoulder.

The Americans lost the battle that day, and Molly was taken prisoner. The wound in her shoulder prevented her from ever using her arm again.

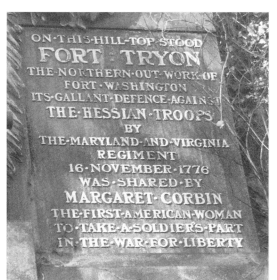

This marker in Fort Tryon Park in New York City calls Margaret Corbin "the first American woman to take a soldier's part in the war for liberty."

Like many other patriots, she paid a high price for liberty.

After the war, Congress awarded Molly a wounded soldier's pension. A special marker honors the part she played in the war.

**Mary Hays** of Pennsylvania was also known as "Molly Pitcher." She married a gunner named John Caspar Hays. When his regiment was sent to fight the British army in New Jersey, Mary went too.

1754?–1821?

Like Margaret Corbin, "Molly" Hays carried water to cool down the cannons. She also nursed wounded men and helped carry them off the battlefield to safety.

On a hot day in June 1778, Mary's husband collapsed during the Battle of Monmouth in New Jersey. Molly held his hand while other soldiers carried him off the field to the army doctor.

When the doctor said John would be all right, Molly remembered her husband's silent cannon. She rushed back to the battlefield.

She knew how to load and fire it and then swab the barrel with a cold, wet sponge before reloading. She'd watched John do it many times.

During the rest of the battle, Molly manned the cannon. She was soon covered with gunpowder, sweat, and smoke.

Suddenly, a British cannonball whizzed right between her legs! Private Joseph Martin saw Molly's skirt and petticoat ripped away by the shot. He could not believe that she was not injured.

He heard her say, "Lucky thing it didn't pass a little higher." Then she went right on firing her husband's cannon.

When the long Battle of Monmouth was over, the soldiers told General Washington about Molly's bravery. The general came to shake Molly's hand and personally thank her for what she'd done.

Today, there is a statue of Mary Hays near her grave in Carlisle, Pennsylvania.

# ★ 9 ★
# DAUGHTERS OF THE AMERICAN REVOLUTION

After many long years of war, the American colonists finally won their fight for independence. In 1783, the British government signed the Treaty of Paris. This treaty recognized the thirteen original colonies as a new nation: the United States of America.

American women had given up many things for the war effort. They boycotted tea and English cloth. They melted their best pewter dishes for bullets. They fought for what they believed in—in schoolrooms and sewing rooms, on battlefields, and sometimes in their own parlors.

One battle-weary British soldier wrote a letter home to his family in England. It read:

*Even in their dresses, the females seem to bid us defiance . . . an officer told Lord Cornwallis . . . that he believed if he had destroyed all the men in North America, we should have enough to do to conquer the women.*

There was no doubt that the Daughters of Liberty had played an important role in the birth of their new country.

Abigail Adams, who later became the nation's second First Lady, proudly wrote to her husband, John:

Abigail Adams

*Publick spirit lives—lives*
*in the bosoms of the Fair Daughters*
*of America, who . . . unite their efforts*
*to reward the patriotick, stimulate the*
*Brave, to alleviate the Burden of War*
*and to show that they are not dismayed*
*by defeats or misfortunes.*

Today, there are still many women patriots. They live in all fifty states and in U.S. territories too. Like the Daughters of Liberty during the American Revolution, these women serve our country as nurses, soldiers, and writers. Some are pilots and politicians. Others serve on the police force or with fire departments.

You may even know some of these women. Perhaps they live in your neighborhood.

They could be your aunts, grandmothers, and sisters. Or even your mom.

Maybe one day soon such a patriot will become the first woman president or vice president of the United States. Perhaps it will be you!

# A PATRIOT TIMELINE

1765      *Mercy Otis Warren* writes letters to fan the flames of patriotism.

1773      *Phillis Wheatley*'s first poems are published. The Boston Tea Party is staged by the Sons of Liberty in Boston Harbor.

1774      *"Mad" Ann Trotter Bailey* becomes a wilderness scout for the patriot militia. Ladies of Edenton, North Carolina, host their tea party.

1775      "The Shot Heard Around the World": war begins at Lexington and Concord. *Prudence Cummings Wright* guards Jewett's Bridge.

1776      The Declaration of Independence is approved by the colonies. *Nancy Ward* helps prevent a massacre. *Betsy Ross* makes flags. *Rebecca Stillwell Willets* guards Beesley's Point. *Margaret Cochran Corbin* is wounded in the battle at Fort Washington.

1777      *Mary Katharine Goddard* prints and distributes the first official copies of the Declaration of Independence. *Sybil Ludington* rallies the New York militia. *Lydia Darragh* saves General Washington's troops from a surprise attack.

| | |
|---|---|
| *Winter* <br> *1777–* <br> *1778* | *Polly Cooper* and the Oneida Indians bring food and medicine to Washington's soldiers at Valley Forge. Martha Washington knits socks for soldiers. |
| *1778* | *Mary Hays* mans a cannon at the Battle of Monmouth. |
| *1779* | *Mammy Kate* rescues Colonel Heard from a British prison. *Nancy Morgan Hart* earns the name "War Woman." |
| *1780* | Following the death of *Esther Reed, Sarah Franklin Bache* delivers over two thousand handmade shirts to George Washington for his army. *Dicey Langston* warns Little Eden of a surprise attack. |
| *1781* | *Emily Geiger* successfully delivers a secret message to patriot general Sumter. *Martha Bell* spies on General Cornwallis. *Elizabeth Hutchinson Jackson* dies while nursing patriot soldiers. *Kerenhappuch Turner* nurses her son back to health. *Deborah Samson* enlists in the Continental Army. |
| *1782* | *Elizabeth "Betty" Zane* saves Fort Henry. |
| *1783* | Benjamin Franklin negotiates the final Treaty of Paris, bringing America's war with Great Britain to an end. |

# AUTHOR'S NOTE

Two years ago, while I stood gazing at the statues of Martha Bell and Kerenhappuch Turner at the Guilford Courthouse National Military Park in North Carolina, I couldn't help wondering about other little-known heroines of the American Revolution.

Determined to tell their stories for a younger generation, I began my research. Unexpectedly, I was faced with the difficult task of choosing which women and girls to include in this collection and which ones to leave out. There were just too many plucky patriots for one book!

I narrowed my choices to the women who inspired me the most. Reluctantly, I omitted many women, like take-charge sisters Rachel and Grace Martin, who disguised themselves as young men and boldly attacked a British messenger. The sisters stole his important dispatches and turned them over to grateful American officers.

There were resourceful women like Elizabeth Hagar (nicknamed "Handy Betty the Blacksmith"), who learned to repair muskets and other weapons for the patriots—including a captured British cannon.

There were generous women like Faith Robinson Trumbull, the wife of the governor of Connecticut. When her minister asked his congregation to make a donation for the patriot troops one Sunday morning, Faith rose from her seat and removed her beautiful red cloak. Touched by Faith's generosity, others donated rings, gold watch chains, and purses filled with money.

Some women, like the incredible Eliza Lucas Pinckney of South Carolina, could easily be the fascinating subject of an entire book. She has been called colonial America's most successful businesswoman. It is said that George Washington even served as a pallbearer at Eliza's well-attended funeral.

I was surprised to discover that women in other countries did what they could to aid the patriot cause. The women of Havana, Cuba, for instance, donated their diamonds to fund General Washington's Continental Army. French women sent uniforms. Spanish women in New Orleans stockpiled clothing, gunpowder, and other provisions for the poorly equipped colonial troops. Even as far west as California, Arizona, and New Mexico, Spanish colonial women sent money and cattle for the cause.

I have tried to be as accurate as possible while telling the stories of these women. This was not always easy. Most of the petticoat patriots were just ordinary citizens. Not much information was recorded about their lives. We don't even know what most of them looked like. In some cases, we don't know when they were born and how or when they died. We can only wonder how long they lived and if they had children or grandchildren.

I hope these true stories of courageous American women will inspire those who read them. The fight for life, liberty, and the pursuit of happiness is never an easy one. Young and old, rich and poor, wives and widows—we would not have won the American Revolution without these patriots in petticoats.

# BIBLIOGRAPHY

*Books*

Baker, Thomas E. *The Monuments at Guilford Courthouse National Military Park, North Carolina.* Pamphlet. Greensboro, N.C.: Guilford Courthouse National Military Park, 1979.

Booth, Sally Smith. *The Women of '76.* New York: Hastings House, 1974.

Buchanan, John. *The Road to Guilford Courthouse: The American Revolution in the Carolinas.* New York: John Wiley and Sons, 1997.

Carrington, Colonel Henry B. *Battles of the American Revolution, 1775–1781.* New York: Promontory Press, 1881.

Chávez, Thomas E. *Spain and the Independence of the United States: An Intrinsic Gift.* Albuquerque: University of New Mexico Press, 2002.

Claghorn, Charles Eugene. *Women Patriots of*

the American Revolution: A Biographical Dictionary. Metuchen, N.J.: Scarecrow Press, 1994.

Commager, Henry Steele, and Richard B. Morris, eds. *The Spirit of 'Seventy-Six: The Story of the American Revolution as Told by Participants.* New York: Bonanza Books, 1983.

Lefler, Hugh T., and William S. Powell. *Colonial North Carolina: A History.* New York: Charles Scribner, 1973.

Lewis, Virgil A. *Life and Times of Ann Bailey: Pioneer Heroine of the Great Kanawha Valley.* 1891. Reprint. Point Pleasant, W.Va.: Discovery Press, 1998.

Norton, Mary Beth. *Liberty's Daughters: The Revolutionary Experience of American Women, 1750–1800.* Ithaca, N.Y.: Cornell University Press, 1996.

Raphael, Ray. *A People's History of the American Revolution: How Common People Shaped the Fight for Independence.* New York: HarperPerennial, 2002.

Smith, Jessie Carney et al., eds. *Black Firsts: 2,000 Years of Extraordinary Achievement.* Detroit, Mich.: Visible Ink Press, 1994.

Wood, Ernie. "Martha Bell Tolled the Woe for Tories." *News and Observer* (Raleigh, N.C.). February 1, 1976.


*Web Sites*

Notable Women Ancestors:
www.rootsweb.com/~nwa

Oneida Nation:
www.oneida-nation.net

West Virginia Division of Culture and History:
www.wvculture.org/history


*Additional Sources*

Cherokee Heritage Museum and Gallery
(Cherokee, N.C.)

Hollis Historical Society (Hollis, N.H.)

Museum of the Cherokee Indian
(Cherokee, N.C.)

# PICTURE CREDITS

Photos courtesy of:
The Athenaeum of Philadelphia (p. 66). © Bettmann/CORBIS (cover, inside front flap, title page, p. 7, pp. 22–23, p. 31, p. 33, pp. 44–45, p. 49, p. 78, p. 83). Bryn Barnard (pp. xii–xiii, pp. 110–111). © CORBIS (p. 56, pp. 104–105). Frick Art Reference Library (p. 65). Getty Images (p. 1 and facing, p. 8, p. 20, p. 25, p. 26, p. 36, p. 37, p. 41, p. 52, pp. 80–81, p. 96, p. 107). © Historical Picture Archive/CORBIS (p. 47). © Lee Snider; Lee Snider/CORBIS (p. 51). The Library of Congress (p. 11, p. 12, p. 21, p. 27, p. 38, p. 102). The Library of Congress, Prints and Photographs Division, HABS, MASS, 9-PEP, 1-1 (p. 54). Mary Evans Picture Library (p. 2, p. 75, p. 87). The Metropolitan Museum of Art (p. 29: Rogers Fund, 1913 [14.26]; p. 30: Catharine Lorillard Wolfe Collection, Wolfe Fund, 1901 [01.20]. All rights reserved.). Mount Vernon Ladies' Association (p. 57). Museum of Fine Arts, Boston (p. 5: petticoat, American, Colonial, mid-18th century, quilted silk satin with cotton lining and cotton drawstring, 267 x 97 cm [105 1/8 x 38 3/16 in], gift of the Misses Aimée and Rosamond Lamb, 59.454; p. 14: John Singleton Copley, American, 1738–1815, *Mrs. James Warren (Mercy Otis)*, about 1763, oil on canvas, 126.05 x 100.33 cm [49 5/8 x 39 1/2 in], bequest of Winslow Warren, 31.212. Photographs © 2003.). National Park Service, Harpers Ferry Center (p. 40, p. 64). Nell Dillon-Ermers (p. 100). Oneida Nation Museum (p. 43). © Owaki—Kulla/CORBIS (p. 34). Picture Collection, The Branch Libraries, The New York Public Library, Astor, Lenox, and Tilden Foundations (p. 60, p. 86, pp. 94–95). © Ronnie Kaufman/ CORBIS (p. 108). Town of Carmel Historical Society (p. 92). West Virginia State Archives (p. 77).

# INDEX

# ABOUT THE AUTHOR

Shirley Raye Redmond fell in love with women's history when she first read Laura Ingalls Wilder's *Little House on the Prairie* books as a child. She went on, she recalls, to read "every biography in the school library, from Abigail Adams and Nellie Bly to all-around athlete Babe Didrikson Zaharias."

As an adult, Shirley Raye became fascinated by the role of women in the American Revolution. "Too often, we overlook the contributions of women in our country's history," Shirley Raye says. "Historians agree that without the support of dedicated colonial women, the colonial men would not have been able to win the Revolutionary War."

Shirley Raye is the author of several nonfiction books for young readers. She and her husband have two grown children and live in Los Alamos, New Mexico.